Common French Phrases

1001+ Everyday Phrases in French
(*written by a French Guy*)

Raphaël Pesquet

Copyright © 2022 Raphaël Pesquet

The content contained within this book may not be reproduced, duplicated or transmitted without direct written permission from the author or the publisher. Under no circumstances will any blame or legal responsibility be held against the publisher, or author, for any damages, reparation, or monetary loss due to the information contained within this book, either directly or indirectly.

Legal Notice : This book is copyright protected. It is only for personal use. You cannot amend, distribute, sell, use, quote or paraphrase any part, or the content within this book, without the consent of the author or publisher.

Disclaimer Notice : Please note the information contained within this document is for educational and entertainment purposes only. All effort has been executed to present accurate, up to date, reliable, complete information. No warranties of any kind are declared or implied. Readers acknowledge that the author is not engaged in the rendering of legal, financial, medical or professional advice. The content within this book has been derived from various sources. Please consult a licensed professional before attempting any techniques outlined in this book

By reading this document, the reader agrees that under no circumstances is the author responsible for any losses, direct or indirect, that are incurred as a result of the use of the information contained within this document, including, but not limited to, errors, omissions, or inaccuracies.

Picture on cover : https://fr.freepik.com/vecteurs-libre/composition-ronde-paris_9462291.htm

Table of Contents

Common French Phrases 1
    How to get the most value out of this book ? 9
    The 3 little tricks to memorize more easily 11
    3 French pronunciation secret to avoid sounding like a tourist . 22
    The 1001+ most common phrases in French 25
        Date and numbers 27
        Telling the time 29
        Days of the week 30
        Months of the year 31
    Make yourself understood 34
        Backup phrases 34
    During a conversation 37
        Words of everyday life 37
        Useful words to build a sentence 39
        Getting to know someone 40
        Weather 42
        Phone call 42
        At the hotel 44
        Useful words at the hotel 47
        Request a service 48
    Taking public transport 50
        Tickets 50
        Take the car 51
        Take the train 54
        Take the bus 57
        Take the cab 58

Take the subway 59
Take the plane 60
Request a direction 62
Food and beverages 64
Food and drinks 64
Meals 66
Order at the restaurant 69
Cooking of the meat 73
Health 74
At the doctor's 74
At the pharmacy 77
At the hospital 79
At the dentist 81
Leisure activities 84
Tourism 84
Interests 85
Sports 89
Shopping 92
Color and sizes 92
Money and payment 95
Useful questions and phrases 98
BONUS: French expressions 104
Congratulations 110

About the author

Hello, my name is Raphaël Pesquet ! I was born, and raised in France (*in a small town near Paris*). I started learning English as a second language when I was 5 years old, my mother encouraged me... and I absolutely loved it !

Today, I am bilingual in French and English and my passion is to teach the French language to people who, like you, want to discover the French language and culture.

Currently, I teach French online and I have already helped more than 250 people to become fluent in French... and I don't intend to stop there ! My goal is to help more than 100'000 people discover France (*its language and culture*). In this book, I will share with you all my tips and methods to help you speak French in everyday life.

We will see real everyday conversations between French people. So, you can be inspired by the questions and answers shared in this book when you come to France or a French-speaking country to travel. So I hope you are motivated, because you are about to dive into French culture ! Let's get started right away.

Introduction

First of all, congratulations ! Today, you have taken action and made a big step towards learning French. Indeed, many people say they would like to learn a new language or discover the French language... but few of them take real and concrete action.

So for that, I really want to congratulate you. As you will see, I put a lot of effort, time and sweat (*and many cups of coffee*) into writing this book so that you can easily and simply discover French phrases that are really USEFUL for communicating in France or in a French speaking country.

Many similar books present far-fetched phrases that you will probably never have to use as a tourist... and even in your entire life, no matter what language you speak ! **The purpose of this book is to give you simple and common phrases that are used in everyday life**. So, if you are traveling in France or in a French-speaking country (*like Quebec or Switzerland*), you will be able to communicate with the locals and talk in French.

In addition, in this book, I will also share with you some elements of French culture outside the clichés. Movies and TV shows like to portray the Frenchman as a man with a mustache, a beret and a baguette under his arm, but at the risk of disappointing you, we are not exactly like that !

But don't worry, the French are friendly and kind. And if you make the effort to speak their language, even with an English accent and a few grammatical mistakes, they will be very pleased and will do everything to help you.

So don't be too hard on yourself. The French language is complicated to learn because it contains many exceptions in its rules. So if a French person hears you say something wrong ? He won't judge you, so don't worry about it.

$97.00 FREE BONUSES

GRAB YOUR FREE BONUSES NOW

- 7 French Short Stories You'll Want to Read
- 14 Common Mistakes In French Made By Beginners
- 21 Daily French Conversations to Learn French
- BONUS : Your Step-By-Step French Study Plan

Scan the QR code to claim your **free** bonus
Or
masterfrenchnow.com/freebonus

How to get the most value out of this book ?

This book is composed of three main parts. Before giving you the most common phrases in everyday French and their translation, I will first talk a little about pronunciation. Don't worry, it will be quick and we will only see the essentials. Even if the accent is important to be understood, I don't think it is necessary to have a "perfect" accent if you want to travel in France or in a French speaking country.

To tell you the truth, even after years of speaking English, I have always kept my "Frenchy" accent, and English speakers like it ! So don't worry, no long boring lessons, we'll just cover the basics.

In addition, to facilitate your learning, I have classified the common phrases by theme, which has two big advantages. The first is that in less than 5 minutes you can read a category of common phrases. So even if you don't have much time, you can learn French in less than 5 minutes a day. The second big advantage of the classification is that if you want to find a sentence quickly, you just have to go to the table of contents, look at the page number of the category you are interested in and go there.

This can be very useful if you are in France or in a French-speaking country and you need to quickly ask for advice, a service or a train ticket for example.
Before we start, you should know one thing : **In France, few people can understand and speak English, that's a fact**. You may be lucky enough to meet someone who understands you, but it's often more difficult to talk and exchange ideas. So having this

guide in your bag can save you !

The 3 little tricks to memorize more easily

For several years, I have been helping English-speaking students learn French. Some learn the language quickly in a few months while others struggle after years. Naturally, because I want to do my job well, I've been digging to find out why there are such differences, and here's what I found... and it has NOTHING to do with intelligence.

Students who become good at French quickly ALL have the same thing in common : they are consistent in their French practice. Every day they progress a little bit. You don't have to spend hours every day, in fact, just 5 or 10 minutes every day is enough. That's the secret. Nothing else.

If you can manage to do only 5 or 10 minutes of French a day for a few months, you will be able to communicate with a French speaker. This may seem simple to you because, after all, 5 or 10 minutes a day isn't much... and yet, most people give up after a few weeks ! So before I reveal the common expressions of everyday French people, I'll give you some tips to keep you going.

Tip #1 : This is a marathon not a sprint

Often, when we start something new in our lives, we are excited and motivated. So we spend hours and hours on our new activity, dive right in and make progress. The problem ? Once the motivation goes down, most people stop.

So, to avoid this problem, I tell my students NOT to work too hard on their French. Yes, this may sound surprising... and at the same time not so much. You know, our brains can only store a limited amount of information per day, so there is no need to "force" learning.

The first rule is to start slowly when learning French. Every day, set aside 5 or 10 minutes to practice and learn French. Don't try to do more at first, just get into the habit of practicing a little each day.

By the way, I strongly recommend that you read this guide several times. In particular, the large section with common phrases is divided into several categories. You can read one category each day, and you'll see that you'll get through this book quickly, and memorize many phrases !

Tip #2 : You can "consume" French in several ways

When I say that you should practice French for 5 to 10 minutes every day, it doesn't mean that you should only read sentences in French !

You can watch Youtube videos with subtitles, you can read short stories written in French with English translation, these are two excellent methods that I recommend to my students who want to learn the language while discovering French culture.

Tip #3 : Read before you sleep

Your brain will consolidate the information you have absorbed during the day at night, while you sleep. So if you want to effectively memorize the French phrases in this book, I invite you to read this guide just before going to bed.

In order not to forget and get into the habit, you can leave this book on your pillow or on your bedside table. This way, as you will see it every day, it will be easier for you to get into the habit.

In general, our brain always looks for the easiest path when it has to do something. Let me give you a concrete example. A long time ago, when I was still a teenager, I had skin problems and I had to apply a cream on my face every night just before going to bed. I had the good idea to put the cream on my bedside table, so I could reach it from my bed, and everything was fine.

But one day, my mother came to put some things away in my room and put my cream on my desk, far from my bed. The result ? I didn't apply my cream anymore. Sometimes I would be in bed and think about the cream, but when I saw it was on my desk and I had to leave my warm bed, I would say to myself, "Oh, never mind, I'll put it on tomorrow. And the next day ? You guessed it : it was the same thing. To get back into the habit of putting that cream on my face before bed, I simply moved the cream from the desk to my nightstand like before.

So I know, this example may seem silly to you, you may think I'm lazy because the cream was only a few feet away... but that's how the brain is, it rejects difficulty in favor of simplicity.

So if you want to make any habit in your life, it's important to simplify your daily routine so that this new habit is easy to adopt. So here I simply recommend that you put this guide on your pillow or by your bed.In general, our brain always looks for the easiest way when it has to do something. Let me give you a concrete example. A long time ago, when I was still a teenager, I had skin problems and I had to apply a cream on my face every night just before going to bed. I had the good reflex to put the cream on my bedside table, so I could reach it from my bed, and everything was fine.

TIP : If you want to easily adopt a new habit, the best way is to link it to an existing habit in your daily life.

Let me give you a concrete example. If you want to practice French for 5 to 10 minutes a day, find a habit in your daily life that you do every day for 5 or 10 minutes.

I like to use the example of coffee or tea. If you drink tea or coffee every day, you can enjoy your hot drink with this book in your hand or a Youtube video on your phone. And since you drink coffee or tea every day, you will easily do your 5 to 10 minutes of French !

Yes, learning a new language can be that easy. As I said, the most important thing is to get into the habit of practicing every day a little bit. If you can do that ? Then you will quickly improve your French.

Another example, a little less traditional but which works great, can be the toilet. Every day you probably go to the toilet, so why not take advantage of it to learn French ? You can leave this book in your toilet to think about it every time you go, I promise you it works really well !

By applying these little tips in your daily life and discovering the phrases in this book every day, French will really become a breeze for you. Okay, now let's go over some French pronunciation rules together. Like I said, this won't be a long and boring course.

I see a lot of books that go into detail... and it's boring ! Science proves that, naturally, by listening to videos and series in French, you will improve your accent without even realizing it. Nevertheless, we will still see some basics together, but they are important enough to make you understand a French person. So without further ado, let's get started.

French pronunciation for beginners

It is easier to learn to speak French for a foreigner than to learn to speak English. Indeed, the English language is composed of 44 phonemes (*which could be compared to sounds*) while the French language has only 36.

On the other hand, in the 36 phonemes of the French language, there are 10 that you won't find in English. So in this chapter we will see how to pronounce them easily. But before we do, I'd like to show you a few mistakes you shouldn't make when pronouncing French. Let's start right away :

The 3 biggest mistakes to avoid when speaking French

Speaking French well is not that complicated. However, there are a few mistakes that can give you a hard time in your French conversations. In this short section, I will present the 3 main mistakes that most beginners make when learning French.

Mistake #1 : The pronunciation of the letter "R"

This mistake has already traumatized thousands of people wishing to learn French around the world... I'm obviously talking about the pronunciation of the letter "R" which is radically different from the English pronunciation.

Here are some French words with the letter "R" :

- Réponse (Answer)
- Râleur (Grumpy)
- Route (Road)

First of all, to pronounce the "R" in French, you must stick the tip of your tongue against the back of your lower front teeth. Then, pretend you are clearing your throat. Like when you are sick and snot falls down your throat, I'm sorry for the comparison, but this way you understand me !

Once you have mastered this weird "grunt", you can try to pronounce French words. So at first it will be difficult, you will tend to pronounce the "R" as in English, and if that is the case, no worries. Most French people will understand you just fine.

However, with practice and listening to French people speak, you will slowly but surely adjust your "R" when you speak French. So don't panic, even if it is complicated at first, it comes with time and practice.

Mistake #2 : The links between words

In French, the liaison consists in pronouncing a final consonant that is normally silent. The liaison joins the consonant at the end of the word to the vowel of the following word. In English too we use liaisons.

For example in "My name is Jack". You don't pronounce the "e" at the end of the word "name", you link it directly, which gives you something like this : "My nam_is Jack". Well, in French it's exactly the same thing !

Here are some examples :

- Vous emportez (You take away)
- Vous en voulez ? (Do you want some ?)
- Il est trop ambitieux. (He is too ambitious)

To learn and detect slurs quickly, you need to be aware of them when you read French text. At first, you need to be alert and even pick up a pen, make the slurs and then pronounce the text. Soon, you will begin to integrate the concept in your mind and you won't even need to make an effort.

Mistake #3 : The silent letters

This mistake is quite deceitful and very present in the French language. In fact, very often, most of the letters at the end of a word are not pronounced or are even ignored.

> **TIP** : A good mnemonic to get by is the acronym "CaReFuL". Indeed, as I told you, most of the letters at the end of the word are not pronounced in French... so it is easier to remember the letters that are pronounced !
>
> The letters that are pronounced most of the time are the consonants present in the word "CaReFuL" so C, R, F and L. In most cases, if the word ends with another letter, then you should not pronounce it.

Of course, since this is the French language, there is always an exception. Here, it is the verbs of the first group that end in -ER. For these verbs, you should not pronounce the "R" at the end because the group of letters -ER forms a particular phoneme that we will see together later. Here are some examples of verbs ending in -ER :

- Manger (Eat)
- Gratter (Scratch)
- Brûler (Burn)

That's it ! These are the 3 main mistakes of the French language. You will probably have a little difficulty avoiding some of them, but once again, don't worry. With time, you'll get it.

I know that it can seem impressive when you see all that you have to learn, you can even feel overwhelmed. Nevertheless, every year millions of people learn French anyway, so you'll get there too !

The pronunciation of vowels

Here is a little table to help you pronounce the vowels :

Sound	Pronunciation	Example in French
a	Like "ah"	Abricot (Apricot)
à	Like "ah"	Voilà (Here you go)
â	Like "ah"	Âme (Soul)
e	Like "er" in "error"	Erreur (Error)
é	Like "hey" without the -y	Épave (Wreck)
è	Like "ai" in "fair"	Père (Father)
i, y	Like "ee" in "meeting"	Citron (Lemon)
o	Like "oh"	Oligarche (Oligarch)

Sound	Pronunciation	Example in French
ô	Like "oh"	Chômage (Unemployment)
u	Say "ee" with your mouth in an o shape	Tumeur (Tumor)
oi	Like "wah"	Oie (Goose)
ou	Like "ou" in "you"	Bijoux (Jewelry)
ai, ei	Like the "e" in "let"	Aigle (Eagle)
au, eau	Like "oh"	Beaucoup (a lot)
eu, œu	Like "er" in "error"	Nœud (Knot)

The pronunciation of consonants

Here is a little table to help you pronounce the consonants :

Sound	Pronunciation	Example in French
ci, ce	Pronounced like an "s".	Cire (Wax)
ca, co	Pronounced like a "k"	Camembert (Famous cheese)
ç	Pronounced like an "s".	Leçon (Lesson)
ch	Pronounced like "sh".	Chat (Cat)

Sound	Pronunciation	Example in French
ga, go	Like the "g" in "gum".	Gamelle (Bowl for animals)
h	It does not pronounce	Haricot (Bean)
j	Like the "s" in "measure".	Joie (Joy)
qu	Pronounced like a "k"	Qualité (Quality)

The main nasal sounds in French

Here is a little table to help you pronounce the nasal sounds in French :

Sound	Pronunciation	Example in French
om, on	Like "on" in "song".	Pont (Bridge)
am, an, em, en	Like "hand" without the "h".	Entier (Integral)
im, in, aim, ain, ein,	Like "one" in "sung"	Faim

un		(Hunger)
oi	Pronounced "wa".	Loi (Law)

3 French pronunciation secret to avoid sounding like a tourist

To improve your French pronunciation quickly, you obviously need to practice and also listen to French people speak. Here are some little-known tips to improve your pronunciation on a daily basis... almost without effort !

Secret #1 : Listen to Radio France

Radio France is a radio that broadcasts only French music. You can put this radio in the background while you drive your car or do your sport for example. You don't need to be 100% focused on the music.

In fact, just by listening to it in the background, your brain will start to recognize pronunciations, letters, words and sentences ! By listening to French songs you expose yourself to the language but also to the culture... and all this in a pleasant way.

Secret #2 : Series and videos

If you are a complete beginner in French, then I recommend you to watch series and videos with English subtitles. This way, you will understand what you are watching, you will discover new words and recognize the ones that appear again and again. In addition, by listening to native French speakers, you will be inspired and retain the pronunciations of the different sounds of the language.

When you are more experienced, you can put videos and series in French with French subtitles. This way, you can work on sentence structure and even spelling.

Secret #3 : Specialized websites

To hear the pronunciation of a specific word, you can use Google Translate or DeepL (which is better in my opinion), many people do it... however I don't recommend it. Even if most of the pronunciations are well done, some are imperfect.

I often advise my students to go to these two little-known sites that I consider to be the best :

- Forvo.com
- Rhinospike.com

These sites have huge databases and give the oral pronunciation in the voice of a native speaker. Thus, you are sure to have a correct pronunciation with all the subtleties that this includes.

End of the introduction

That's it ! We just finished the part on pronunciation. We've seen together how you can quickly improve your French pronunciation by following a few simple rules and tricks. You can come back to this chapter from time to time to refresh your memory on the pronunciation of French words.

Now we will look at some everyday phrases that you can use when speaking to a French person. The phrases are categorized and sub-categorized so that you can find them more easily. I hope you are motivated... because you are about to discover the language of the French !

The 1001+ most common phrases in French

Before I begin, I would like to give you a warning. In many books teaching French, a simplified phonetic notation is given to help you pronounce the phrase or word in question. To be honest, I don't think this is a good method, and I'll tell you why.

This pronunciation aid is a bad habit for English speakers who want to learn French. Indeed, by reading this pronunciation you will pronounce the French word with an English accent.

And if you take this bad habit, then you will have a strong English accent when you speak French... and it will even sound a bit cliché for the French !

So here's my recommendation, instead of trying to pronounce French words with an English accent and phonetic inscription, here's what I recommend : read the sentences I'm going to share with you, look at the spelling, the structure as well as the grammar. If you want to improve your pronunciation, download the FREE audio training I shared at the beginning of this book.

Don't force yourself to memorize them, the goal is to familiarize yourself with the French language and unconsciously, your brain will start to remember the words and then the sentences.

Then, for the pronunciation, the best is to watch videos or series with French subtitles. YouTube videos are excellent for example because they feature everyday situations. So in combination with this book it's perfect because you will recognize (*thanks to the subtitles*) the sentences that you have seen in this guide and you will have their perfect pronunciation by a native.

I highly recommend this learning method because it allows you to discover French and its culture while having fun.

Date and numbers

Numbers

Zéro
Zero

Un
One

Deux
Two

Trois
Three

Quatre
Four

Cinq
Five

Six
Six

Sept
Seven

Huit
Eight

Neuf
Nine

Dix
Ten

Onze
Eleven

Douze
Twelve

Treize
Thirteen

Quatorze
Fourteen

Quinze
Fifteen

Seize
Sixteen

Dix-sept
Seventeen

Dix-huit
Eighteen

Dix-neuf
Nineteen

Vingt Twenty	Vingt-et-un Twenty-one
Vingt-deux Twenty-two	Vingt-trois Twenty-three
Vingt-quatre Twenty-four	Vingt-cinq Twenty-five
Trente Thirty	Quarante Forty
Cinquante Fifty	Soixante Sixty
Soixante-dix Seventy	Quatre-vingts Eighty
Quatre-vingt-dix Ninety	Cent One hundred
Mille A thousand	

Telling the time

TIP : There are many ways to tell the time in French, if you want a simple, no-fuss way to tell any time, here's what you should say as an example.

For time 15h45 :

"Il est" + Number of hours + "heures" + Number of minutes
Il est + 15 + heures + 45
Il est 15 heures 45.

This is the easiest way to tell the time, and by telling it this way you are sure to be understood by all French people. In this chapter, I will still share with you more elegant and common ways to tell the time... even if they are a bit more difficult to learn !

Quelle heure est-il ?
What time is it ?

Il est quelle heure ?
What time is it ?

Il est une heure.
It's one o'clock.

Il est deux heures.
It's two o'clock.

Il est quatre heures et quart.
It is quarter past four.

Il est cinq heures et demie.
It is half past five.

Il est six heures moins le quart.
It is a quarter to six.

Il est neuf heures moins vingt.
It is twenty minutes to nine.

Il est trois heures cinq.
It is five past three.

Il est huit heures du soir.
It's 8 p.m.

Il est midi.
It's noon.

Il est minuit.
It's midnight.

Il est quatorze heures quinze.
It is 2 :15 p.m.

Il est quinze heures trente-cinq.
It's 3 :35 p.m.

Rule : Officially, "the quarters", "the halves" and "minus the quarter" must only be used for the hours of the morning, thus from 1 to 12. Nevertheless, the majority of the French pronounce them all the same for the afternoon.

Days of the week

Lundi
Monday

Mardi
Tuesday

Mercredi
Wednesday

Jeudi
Thursday

Vendredi
Friday

Samedi
Saturday

Dimanche
Sunday

On est lundi
It's Monday

La semaine
The week

La semaine prochaine.
Next week.

La semaine dernière.
Last week

On se voit la semaine prochaine.
See you next week.

Je travaille le lundi.
I work on Mondays.

Je vous retrouve à midi.
I will meet you at noon.

Demain
Tomorrow

Hier
Yesterday

La veille (*plus formel*)
Yesterday (*more formal*)

À quelle heure le magasin ouvre-t-il ?
What time does the store open ?

À quelle heure le soleil se couche ?
What time does the sun set ?

On est quel jour ?
What day is it ?

Ma réunion est dans dix minutes.
My meeting is in ten minutes.

Quelle heure est-il s'il vous plaît ?
What time is it, please ?

À quelle heure est le rendez-vous ?
What time is the appointment ?

Months of the year

Janvier
January

Février
February

Mars
March

Avril
April

Mai
May

Juin
June

Juillet
July

Août
August

Septembre
September

Octobre
October

Novembre
November

Décembre
December

Hiver
Winter

Printemps
Spring

Été
Summer

Automne
Fall

Une année
A year

L'année prochaine
Next year

L'année dernière
Last year

Le Nouvel An
The New Year

Les vacances de janvier.
January Holidays.

Je pars le mois prochain.
I'm leaving next month.

J'arrive le mois prochain.
I'm coming next month.

Quand est ton anniversaire ?
When is your birthday ?

How to say a date in French ?

Saying a date in French is a little different from English in the structure. Indeed, we say first the number of the day then the month. Here is a concrete example :

Nous avons rendez-vous le **18 octobre.**
We have an appointment on **October 18th.**

So here is the template to say a date in French :

"Le" + Number of the day + Name of the month

Le + 18 + Octobre
Le 18 Octobre
October 18th.

Make yourself understood

Sometimes it can be difficult to make yourself understood, or to understand what someone is saying to you... and that's perfectly normal ! With the stress or the accent of some French people, you may have trouble making yourself understood.

In this quick chapter, I'll give you a few phrases to help you make yourself understood. If you are worried about losing your temper when you speak to a French person... then, you'll love this part !

Backup phrases

Je ne comprends pas ce que vous dites.
I don't understand what you are saying.

Pouvez-vous parler plus lentement ?
Can you speak more slowly ?

Parlez-vous anglais ?
Do you speak English ?

Pouvez-vous parler anglais ?
Can you speak English ?

Je ne comprends pas.
I don't understand.

Merci beaucoup pour votre aide.
Thank you very much for your help.

Je parle seulement l'anglais.
I only speak English.

Vous pouvez traduire en anglais ?
Can you translate it into English ?

Est-ce que quelqu'un parle anglais ici ?
Does anyone here speak English ?

Je parle un petit peu français.
I speak a little French.

Vous pouvez me traduire ce mot ?
Can you translate this word for me ?

Comment dit-on "exemple" en français ?
How do you say "example" in French ?

Pouvez-vous répéter s'il vous plaît ?
Could you repeat that please ?

Pouvez-vous l'écrire s'il vous plaît ?
Can you please write it down ?

Pourriez-vous m'aider ?
Can you help me ?

Qu'est-ce que cela signifie en anglais ?
What does this mean in English ?

Je suis américain.	Je suis anglais.
I am American.	I am British.

Est-ce que je dis ce mot correctement ?
Am I saying this word correctly ?

C'est la première fois que je viens en France !

This is my first time in France !

During a conversation

The French and politeness

As a general rule, the French are very polite and like to take it easy when they speak. We don't seek confrontation, we are more friendly.

We are very fussy about politeness. Don't panic either, if you are a foreigner we will forgive you without worry. In this chapter I will give you some tips and common phrases for your conversations with French speakers.

Words of everyday life

Oui
Yes

Non
No

Peut-être
Maybe

S'il vous plaît
Please

Merci
Thank you

De rien
You are welcome

Pardon
Sorry

Excusez-moi.
I'm sorry.

Entrez s'il vous plaît.
Please come in.

Bienvenue
Welcome

Je suis en retard.
I'm running late.

Merci pour votre patience.
Thank you for your patience.

J'ai faim.

J'ai soif.

I am hungry.

Ce n'est pas grave.
That's okay.

Où sont les toilettes ?
Where is the toilet ?

Bien sûr
Of course

Bon anniversaire
Happy Birthday

À mon avis
In my opinion

Voilà
That's it

On y va ?
Shall we go ?

I'm thirsty.

J'attends mes amis.
I'm waiting for my friends.

Tout à fait
Absolutely

Ça marche
It works

Du coup
As a result

Fais voir
Let me see

N'importe quoi
Nonsense

Je t'aime
I love you

Useful words to build a sentence

Qui
Who

Quoi
What

Quand
When

Où
Where

Dans
In

Dedans
Inside

Près
Near

Loin
Far away

Gauche
Left

Droite
Right

Derrière
Behind

À côté
Beside

Devant
Front

À l'intérieur
Inside

À l'extérieur
Outside

À la vôtre !
Cheers !

Getting to know someone

Bonjour je m'appelle Jean, et vous ?
Hello my name is Jean, and you ?

What is your name ?
Je m'appelle Jean Dujardin.

My name is Jean Dujardin.
Comment vous appelez-vous ?

Comment allez-vous ?
How are you ?

Je vais bien, merci de demander.
I'm fine, thanks for asking.

Vous avez quel âge ?	J'ai 32 ans.
How old are you ?	I am 32 years old.

Vous venez de quel pays ?
What country are you from ?

Je suis Canadien.	Je suis Français.
I am Canadian.	I am French.

Vous habitez dans quelle ville ?
What city do you live in ?

Est-ce que vous êtes marié ?
Are you married ?

Je suis célibataire.
I am single.

Je suis en couple.
I am in a relationship.

Avez-vous des frères et sœurs ?
Do you have brothers and sisters ?

Oui, j'ai un frère et je suis l'aîné.
Yes, I have a brother and I am the oldest.

Quel est votre métier ?   Je suis ingénieur.
What is your job ?   I am an engineer.

Quel est votre sport préféré ?
What is your favorite sport ?

Avez-vous un animal de compagnie ?
Do you have a pet ?

Oui, nous avons deux chiens et un chat.
Yes, we have two dogs and a cat.

Prenez soin de vous.
Please take care of yourself.

Merci pour les informations.
Thank you for the information.

Weather

Quel temps fait-il aujourd'hui ?
What is the weather like today ?

Il fait chaud.
It is hot.

Quelle est la météo de demain ?
What is the weather forecast for tomorrow ?

Il fait froid.
It is cold.

Il caille. (*moins formel*)
It's freezing. (*less formal*)

Le ciel est couvert.
It's cloudy.

Il y a du vent.
It's windy.

Il pleut.
It is raining.

Il y a du soleil.
It's sunny.

Il neige.
It's snowing.

Phone call

The telephone code for France is 33.

So if you want someone to call you from abroad, they will have to type +33 before dialing your number to reach you.

Où puis-je passer un coup de téléphone ?
Where can I make a phone call ?

Combien ça coûte d'appeler les États-Unis ?
How much does it cost to call the United States ?

Quel est l'indicatif téléphonique des États-Unis ?
What is the US area code ?

J'aimerais appeler à la maison.
I would like to call home.

J'aimerais passer un coup de fil.
I would like to make a phone call.

Quel est votre numéro de téléphone ?
What is your phone number ?

J'aimerais acheter un téléphone portable.
I would like to buy a cell phone.

J'aimerais acheter une sim.
I would like to buy a sim.
(you need this if you want to call and send sms)

Bonjour, c'est qui ?
Hello, who is this ?

Mon numéro est le : …
My number is : …

J'aimerais parler à Monsieur Dujardin.
I would like to speak to Monsieur Dujardin.

Bonjour, c'est Jean.
Hello, this is Jean.

Un moment s'il vous plaît.
One moment please.

Vous êtes dans la file d'attente, veuillez patienter, quelqu'un va bientôt prendre votre appel.
You are in the queue, please wait, someone will take your call soon.

Souhaitez-vous laisser un message ?
Would you like to leave a message ?

Je ne peux pas appeler le numéro.
I can't call the number.

At the hotel

Important : If you want to book a hotel or Airbnb in Paris, it is important to do so in advance. Paris is one of the most touristy cities in the world, and hotels and short-term rentals fill up quickly. Make your reservation at least a few weeks before your arrival in France.

Vous connaissez un bon hôtel ?
Do you know a good hotel ?

Pourriez-vous me conseiller un hôtel abordable ?
Can you recommend an affordable hotel ?

Bonjour. J'ai fait une réservation.
Hello. I have made a reservation.

J'ai une réservation au nom de "Dujardin".
I have a reservation in the name of "Dujardin".

Mon nom de famille est Dujardin.
My last name is Dujardin.

Mon prénom est Jean.
My first name is Jean.

J'ai réservé une chambre pour quatre personnes.
I reserved a room for four people.

Je n'ai pas de réservation. Avez-vous des chambres disponibles ?
I do not have a reservation. Do you have any rooms available ?

Vous avez une chambre ?
Do you have a room ?

J'ai fait la réservation en ligne.
I made the reservation online.

Je voudrais une chambre pour trois personnes.
I would like a room for three people.

Je voudrais deux lits séparés.
I would like two twin beds.

Je voudrais un lit pour deux personnes.
I would like a double bed.

Avez-vous un service d'étage ?
Do you have room service ?

Quel est le prix par nuit ?
What is the price per night ?

Quel est le prix par semaine ?
What is the price per week ?

Avez-vous une autre chambre un peu moins chère ?
Do you have another room that is a little cheaper ?

À quelle heure devons-nous rendre la chambre ?
What time is check out ?

Est-ce qu'il y a une réduction pour les enfants ?
Is there a discount for children ?

Pouvez-vous m'aider avec mes valises ?
Can you help me with my luggage ?

Je voudrais payer avec ma carte de crédit ?
I would like to pay with my credit card ?

Tout est compris ?
Is everything included ?

Il faut libérer sa chambre avant midi.
Check out is before noon.

Quel est mon numéro de chambre ?
What is my room number ?

Il y a un problème avec l'eau chaude.
There is a problem with the hot water.

La télévision ne fonctionne pas.
The TV is not working.

Le wifi ne marche pas.
The wifi doesn't work.

Puis-je avoir une couverture supplémentaire ?
Can I have an extra blanket ?

Où puis-je garer ma voiture ?
Where can I park my car ?

Je peux voir la chambre s'il vous plaît ?
Can I see the room please ?

Est-ce que la chambre a... ?
Does the room have... ?

Useful words at the hotel

Douche   Bain

Shower   Bath

Une télévision   Une belle vue.
TV   A nice view.

La climatisation   Le chauffage
Air conditioning   Heating

Request a service

Pouvez-vous m'aider ?
Can you help me ?

Pourriez-vous m'indiquer la station essence la plus proche ?
Can you tell me the nearest gas station ?

Avez-vous vu ... ?
Have you seen ... ?

J'ai oublié mon argent, vous prenez la carte de crédit ?
I forgot my money, do you take the credit card ?

Pouvez-vous m'aider à contacter ... ?
Can you help me to contact ... ?

Pourrais-je avoir de l'eau s'il vous plaît ?
Could I have some water please ?

Pouvez-vous me filer un coup de main avec ... ?
Can you give me a hand with ... ?

Où est le commissariat le plus proche ?
Where is the nearest police station ?

Pouvez-vous m'indiquer la direction de ... ?
Can you give me directions to ... ?

Pouvez-vous m'aider à nettoyer ?
Can you help me clean ?

Pouvons-nous avoir l'addition ?
Can we have the bill ?

Puis-je emprunter ... ?
Can I borrow ... ?

Comment pouvons-nous monter en haut de la tour Eiffel ?
How do we get to the top of the Eiffel Tower ?

Puis-je appeler avec votre téléphone ?
Can I call you on your phone ?

Pouvez-vous nous prendre en photo ?
Can you take a picture of us ?

Pouvons-nous avoir le menu du restaurant ?
Can we have the restaurant menu ?

Vous reste-t-il encore des places ?
Are there any seats left ?

Pouvez-vous mettre de la musique ?
Can you put on some music ?

Avez-vous de la monnaie ?
Do you have any change ?

Taking public transport

Tickets

Première classe.
First class.

Seconde classe.
Second class.

Un tarif de groupe.
A group rate.

Un ticket électronique.
An electronic ticket.

Combien coûte un ticket ?
How much does a ticket cost ?

Puis-je commander un ticket ?
Can I order a ticket ?

Puis-je réutiliser ce ticket ?
Can I reuse this ticket ?

Ce ticket est-il encore valide ?
Is this ticket still valid ?

Je voudrais un billet pour un aller simple.
I would like a one-way ticket.

Je voudrais un billet aller-retour s'il vous plaît.
I would like a round trip ticket please.

Est-ce que ce ticket est remboursable ?
Is this ticket refundable ?

Jusqu'à quand ce ticket est-il valide ?
Until when is this ticket valid ?

Puis-je commander un ticket en ligne ?
Can I order a ticket online ?

À quelle station je dois descendre ?
At which station do I get off ?

Take the car

Be careful when you rent a car !

Many traveler friends have had some problems with car rental companies (*not only French*). Indeed, in this industry "scams" are common.

Renters may tell you that you have damaged the car and ask you for money. When you rent a car, I invite you to take a video or a picture before you even put the keys in the ignition !

That way, if there is a problem, you can show the video. It really does take 1 minute, and it can save you a lot of trouble.

Une voiture
A car

Le frein
The brake

Le boîtier de vitesse
The gearbox

Le siège conducteur
The driver's seat

Le siège passage
The passenger seat

Le clignotant
The turn signal

Le klaxon
The horn

Le volant
The steering wheel

J'aimerais louer une voiture.
I would like to rent a car.

Combien pour louer cette voiture ?
How much does it cost to rent this car ?

L'assurance est-elle comprise ?
Is the insurance included ?

Faut-il verser un acompte ?
Do I have to pay a deposit ?

Est-ce que j'ai besoin d'un permis de conduire international ?
Do I need an international driving license ?

Je conduis de Paris à Marseille.
I drive from Paris to Marseille.

Cette voiture est-elle équipée d'un GPS ?
Is this car equipped with a GPS ?

Je ne peux pas faire démarrer la voiture.
I can't start the car.

La radio ne fonctionne pas.
The radio doesn't work.

Je n'arrive pas à passer la marche arrière.
I can't get it into reverse.

Quel est le modèle de cette voiture ?
What is the model of this car ?

Je vais rouler pendant 450 kilomètres.
I will ride for 450 kilometers.

Dois-je faire le plein d'essence avant de la rendre ?
Do I have to fill up with gas before I return it ?

Je vais manquer d'essence.
I'm running out of gas.

Quel type d'essence dois-je mettre dans cette voiture ?
What kind of gas should I put in this car ?

Quel est le numéro de la dépanneuse ?
What is the number of the tow truck ?

Mon pneu est crevé.
My tire is flat.

Did you know that ?

In France we don't use the unit of measurement "miles", we use kilometers, which is a little different. Here is the conversion :

1 Mile = 1.60 Kilomètre

This is important to know because the signage as well as your dashboard will obviously be in kilometers.

Take the train

In France there are four major railway stations :

- La Gare Montparnasse.
- La Gare Saint-Lazare.
- La Gare du Nord.
- La Gare de l'Est.

There are also many types of trains.

The RER - The network of trains around Paris
The Ouigo - The cheap train network for the big cities of France.
The TGV - The high speed train for long trips

In summary : To get around the capital you will probably take the metro for short trips and the RER for longer ones. If you want to visit several big cities in France, I recommend you to take a OuiGo. If you plan in advance, you can get tickets at very good prices.

Un voyageur
A passenger

Une station de gare
A station

Un billet de train
A train ticket

Un guichet
A ticket counter

Le départ
The departure

L'arrivé
The arrival

Côté allée
Alley side

Côté fenêtre
Window side

Deux places côte à côte
Two seats side by side

Un billet remboursable
One refundable ticket

Un train direct
A direct train

Le numéro de siège
The seat number

La voiture du train
The car of the train

Y a-t-il une correspondance ?
Is there a connection ?

Où se trouve la gare ?
Where is the station ?

Puis-je avoir un remboursement ?
Can I get a refund ?

À quelle heure part le train pour Paris ?
At what time does the train leave for Paris ?

Est-ce que ce train vient de Paris ?

Does this train come from Paris ?

Quel train dois-je prendre pour aller à Paris ?
Which train do I have to take to get to Paris ?

Sur quelle voie dois-je aller pour prendre mon train ?
On which track do I have to go to take my train ?

Il faut composter son billet.
You have to punch your ticket.

Combien de temps dure le trajet ?
How long is the journey ?

Cette place est déjà prise, désolé.
This seat is already taken, sorry.

Où est le wagon-restaurant ?
Where is the dining car ?

Est-ce que je dois changer de train ?
Do I have to change trains ?

Est-ce que le train part à l'heure ?
Does the train leave on time ?

Est-ce que c'est un train direct ?
Is it a direct train ?

Pardon, je pense que c'est ma place.
Sorry, I think this is my seat.

Le train est en retard.
The train is late.

Puis-je déposer mes bagages ?
Can I drop my luggage off ?

Take the bus

Une gare routière
A bus station

Où est l'arrêt de bus ?
Where is the bus stop ?

Ce bus va bien à Paris ?
Is this bus going to Paris ?

À quelle heure est le prochain bus ?
What time is the next bus ?

When will the next bus arrive ?
Quand arrivera le prochain bus ?

Je monte dans le bus.
I get on the bus.

Où est-ce que je peux acheter un billet ?
Where can I buy a ticket ?

Est-ce que ce bus va à Bordeaux ?
Does this bus go to Bordeaux ?

Le bus arrive bientôt à Bordeaux.
The bus arrives soon in Bordeaux.

Est-ce qu'il y a un bus pour Nice ?
Is there a bus to Nice ?

Où est l'arrêt de bus le plus proche ?
Where is the nearest bus stop ?

Pourriez-vous me dire où je dois descendre ?
Could you tell me where I should get off ?

Le prochain arrêt, s'il vous plaît.
The next stop, please.

Est-ce que j'aurai besoin de changer de bus ?
Will I need to change buses ?

Take the cab

Où est-ce que je peux trouver un taxi ?
Where can I find a cab ?

Pourriez-vous m'appeler un taxi ?
Could you call me a cab ?

C'est combien pour aller en ville ?
How much does it cost to go to the city ?

Pouvez-vous nous amener à cette adresse ?
Can you take us to this address ?

Je voudrais aller à l'aéroport s'il vous plaît.
I would like to go to the airport please.

Je suis pressé.
I am in a hurry.

Je voudrais un prix fixe pour ce trajet.
I would like a fixed price for this trip.

Pouvez-vous rouler plus doucement s'il vous plaît ?
Can you please drive more slowly ?

Pouvez-vous mettre un peu de musique ?
Can you put on some music ?

Pourriez-vous m'emmener à cet hôtel ?
Could you take me to this hotel ?

Attendez ici, s'il vous plaît
Wait here, please.

Arrêtez ici, s'il vous plaît
Stop here, please.

J'aimerais aller à la Gare du Nord, s'il vous plaît.
I'd like to go to the North Station, please.

Je voudrais réserver un taxi pour demain à 20 heures.
I would like to book a cab for tomorrow at 8 pm.

Take the subway

Est-ce que vous vendez un carnet de tickets ?
Do you sell a book of tickets ?

À quelle station faut-il descendre pour voir la tour Eiffel ?
Which station do I have to get off at to see the Eiffel Tower ?

Des contrôleurs vont vérifier vos billets.
Ticket inspectors will check your tickets.

Est-ce que je suis dans le bon sens pour aller à Levallois-Perret ?
Am I going the right way to go to Levallois-Perret ?

Quand arrivera le prochain métro ?
When will the next metro arrive ?

Où est le plan du métro ?
Where is the metro map ?

Quelle ligne dois-je prendre pour arriver au Champ-de-Mars ?
Which line should I take to get to the Champ-de-Mars ?

Quand est le prochain arrêt ?
When is the next stop ?

Take the plane

Classe économique   Classe affaires
Economy Class   Business class

La porte d'embarquement
The boarding gate

Commandant de bord
Flight commander

L'enregistrement
The check-in

On décolle bientôt ?
Are we taking off soon ?

Le compartiment à bagages est plein.
The luggage compartment is full.

Excusez-moi, je pense que c'est mon siège.
Excuse me, I think this is my seat.

Je n'aime pas les turbulences.
I don't like turbulence.

Quel est mon numéro de vol ?
What is my flight number ?

Je voudrais réserver une place sur le vol.
I would like to reserve a seat on the flight.

J'ai des bagages enregistrés.
I have checked luggage.

Est-ce qu'il y a une escale ?
Is there a stopover ?

Est-ce que je dois changer d'avion ?
Do I have to change planes ?

Est-ce qu'il y a un vol pour Marseille ?
Is there a flight to Marseille ?

Est-ce que ce vol est direct ?
Is this flight direct ?

À quelle heure l'avion arrive ?

What time does the plane arrive ?

Le vol pour Paris a été annulé.
The flight to Paris has been canceled.

Je me suis enregistré en ligne.
I checked in online.

Embarquement dans 15 minutes.
Boarding in 15 minutes.

Request a direction

Une avenue
An avenue

Un boulevard
A boulevard

Un pont
A bridge

L'Église
The Church

La marie
The town hall

Le lycée
The high school

La bibliothèque
The library

Le centre commercial
The mall

À droite
To the right

À gauche
To the left

Tout droit
Straight ahead

La première à gauche
First left

La troisième rue à droite.
Third street on the right.

En face de
In front of

À côté de
Next to

Au bout de l'avenue.
At the end of the avenue.

Pouvons-nous y aller à pied ?
Can we walk there ?

C'est à quinze minutes d'ici.
It's fifteen minutes from here.

Quelle est la meilleure route pour aller à Paris ?
What is the best way to get to Paris ?

Où se trouve la boulangerie la plus proche ?
Where is the nearest bakery ?

Où est la gare s'il vous plaît ?
Where is the train station, please ?

Pouvez-vous m'indiquer la rue du Général de Gaulle ?
Can you tell me which street is Général de Gaulle ?

Où puis-je me garer s'il vous plaît ?
Where can I park, please ?

Où est le parking le plus proche ?
Where is the nearest parking lot ?

Comment puis-je aller aux Champs-Élysées ?
How can I get to the Champs-Élysées ?

Savez-vous où est la tour Eiffel ?
Do you know where the Eiffel Tower is ?

Prenez la rue à droite, ensuite allez jusqu'à l'école puis tournez à gauche.
Take the street on the right, then go to the school and turn left.

Traversez le pont et tournez à gauche, vous devriez voir le magasin.
Cross the bridge and turn left, you should see the store.

Food and beverages

Food in France is super important !

The French are bon vivants, and food is in our DNA. In France you will find many restaurants with different themes. Moreover, you also have a lot of choices at the supermarket. So if you want to treat yourself... **France is the perfect place !**

Food and drinks

Une bouteille de vin rouge
A bottle of red wine

Le cidre
The cider

Les ailes de poulet
Chicken wings

Les moules
Mussels

Le pain
The bread

L'eau plate
Still water

La carte de vins
The wine list

Les escargots
Snails

La choucroute
Sauerkraut

La bière
The beer

L'eau pétillante
Sparkling water

Avec des glaçons
On the rocks

C'est délicieux
It is delicious

Un plat
A main course

Un apéritif
An appetizer

Une collation
A snack

J'ai faim.
I'm hungry.

L'assaisonnement est parfait.
The seasoning is perfect.

Une entrée
An appetizer

Un dessert
A dessert

La pause-café
Coffee break

J'ai soif.
I'm thirsty.

Je me régale.
I love it.

Pourrais-je avoir du sel ?
Could I have some salt ?

Comment s'appelle ce plat ?
What is the name of this dish ?

La présentation est magnifique
The presentation is beautiful

Pourrais-je en avoir davantage ?
Could I have some more ?

Pourrais-je avoir du poivre ?
Could I have some pepper ?

C'est vraiment appétissant.
It's really appetizing.

For tips in restaurants : In some countries, especially Canada, tipping is almost mandatory. In France this is not the case. Waiters will always appreciate a small tip of a few euros (*1 or 2€*). On the other hand, nowadays, many French people do not leave a tip.

If you want to leave a tip, you can leave a coin on the table where you ate and then go pay at the counter.

Meals

Did you know that ? The French enjoy a sweet breakfast. We often find pastries, jam and bread with butter accompanied by hot chocolate or coffee.

Petit-déjeuner   Déjeuner
Breakfast   Lunch

Le quatre-heures   Dîner
Four o'clock snack   Dinner

Une soupe   La salade
Soup   Salad

J'aimerais un chocolat chaud s'il vous plaît.
I would like a hot chocolate please.

Avez-vous des croissants et des pains au chocolat ?
Do you have croissants and bread with chocolate filling ?

J'aime le pain avec de la confiture.
I like bread with jam.

Avez-vous un sandwich jambon beurre ?
Do you have a ham and butter sandwich ?

Quelle est la recommandation du chef ?
What does the chef recommend ?

J'aimerais du vin blanc.
I would like some white wine.

Pourrais-je avoir une assiette de fromages ?
Could I have a cheese plate ?

Je vous prendrais un café avec mon dessert s'il vous plaît.
I'll have coffee with my dessert please.

Avez-vous choisi ce que vous voulez ?
Have you chosen what you want ?

Qu'aimeriez-vous ?
What would you like ?

Je prendrais bien un repas léger.
I would like to have a light meal.

À quelle heure mange-t-on ?
What time do we eat ?

On mange quoi ?
What are we eating ?

Oui, j'en veux un petit s'il vous plaît.
Yes, I'd like a small one please.

Je suis allergique à…
I'm allergic to...

Je fais un régime.
I am on a diet.

Est-ce que je peux me resservir ?
Can I take more ?

C'est vraiment succulent.
It's really tasty.

Vous pouvez me conseiller un bon restaurant ?

Can you recommend a good restaurant ?

Un buffet à volonté.
An all-you-can-eat buffet.

Je cherche un bar où passer la soirée.
I'm looking for a bar to spend the evening.

Order at the restaurant

Ordering in a French restaurant – conversation :

Serveur : Bonjour, vous avez réservé ?
Waiter : Hello, do you have a reservation ?

Clients : Non, vous avez encore de la place ?
Clients : No, do you still have room ?

Serveur : Oui, bien sûr. Pour combien de personnes ?
Waiter : Yes, of course. For how many people ?

Clients : Nous sommes deux.
Clients : There are two of us.

Serveur : Suivez-moi, je vais vous installer.
Waiter : Follow me, I will install you.

Serveur : Cette table vous convient ?
Waiter : Is this table suitable for you ?

Clients : Oui, parfait !
Clients : Yes, perfect !

Serveur : Parfait, installez-vous, j'arrive avec les menus.
Waiter : Perfect, settle down, I'm coming with the menus.

Serveur : Voici les menus, je reviens dans 5 minutes pour les boissons.
Waiter : Here are the menus, I'll be back in 5 minutes for the drinks.

Clients : Parfait, merci beaucoup.
Clients : Perfect, thank you very much.

Serveur : Vous voulez des boissons ?
Waiter : You'll have drinks ?

Clients : Oui, un Coca-cola et un Orangina.
Clients : Yes, a Coke and an Orangina.

Serveur : Parfait, avez- vous déjà choisi votre entrée ?
Waiter : Perfect, have you already chosen your starter ?

Clients : Oui, nous prendrons du foie gras s'il vous plaît.
Clients : Yes, we'll have some foie gras please.

Serveur : Parfait, c'est noté !
Waiter : Perfect, I got it !

Je voudrais le menu à 16 euros.
I would like the 16 euro menu.

Comment trouvez-vous votre steak frites ?
How do you like your steak frites ?

Je vais vous prendre un café s'il vous plaît.
I'll get you a coffee please.

Qu'est-ce que vous recommander ?
What would you recommend ?

J'ai réservé une table pour quatre personnes.
I have reserved a table for four people.

Une table pour trois personnes s'il vous plaît.
A table for three please.

Peut-on avoir la carte s'il vous plaît ?
Can we have the menu, please ?

Un repas avec une entrée, un plat et un dessert.

A three-course meal.

Quel est le plat du jour ?
What's today's special ?

Je voudrais de l'eau.
I'd like some water.

Avez-vous un menu en anglais ?
Do you have a menu in English ?

Est-ce possible de prendre des plats à emporter ?
Is it possible to order take out ?

Je n'ai pas commandé ça. J'ai pris …
I didn't order this. I had…

Acceptez-vous des cartes de crédit ?
Do you take credit cards ?

Est-ce que vous servez du vin au verre ?
Do you serve wine by the glass ?

En entrée, je voudrais…
For the starter, I would like…

Pour le plat, je vais prendre…
For the main dish, I will have…

En dessert, je voudrais…
For dessert, I would like…

Où sont les toilettes, s'il vous plaît ?
Where is the toilet, please ?

Vous avez choisi ?
Have you chosen ?

Est-ce que vous voulez des boissons ?

Would you like some drinks ?

Je vais prendre un jus d'orange, s'il vous plaît.
I'll have an orange juice, please.

Je vais prendre un coca, s'il vous plaît.
I'll have a coke, please.

Je vais prendre une pression, s'il vous plaît.
I'll have a beer, please.

Je suis allergique aux noix.
I am allergic to nuts.

Est-ce que vous voulez une entrée ?
Would you like an appetizer ?

Je vais prendre le poulet au curry, s'il vous plaît.
I'll have the chicken curry, please.

Je voudrais une glace au chocolat, s'il vous plaît.
I would like a chocolate ice cream, please.

Nous sommes prêts à commander.
We are ready to order.

Avez-vous des plats végétariens ?
Do you have any vegetarian dishes ?

Allez-y, je vous écoute
Go ahead, I'm listening.

Cooking of the meat

Quelle cuisson souhaitez-vous pour votre viande ?
How do you want your meat cooked ?

À point
Medium

Bleu
Blue

Carbonnisée
Browned

Bien cuit
Well done

Saignant
Rare

Health

France and its free health care system

It may depend on your situation, but in general if something happens to you in France and you are taken to the hospital, rest assured that you will not have to pay a bill of several thousand euros.

Indeed, **France works on a solidarity model, and most of the care is paid for by the taxpayer.** We pay a lot of taxes, but we have some advantages !

At the doctor's

Make a doctor's appointment

Patient : Bonjour, je souhaite prendre rendez-vous avec le docteur Dujardin.
Patient : Hello, I would like to make an appointment with Dr. Dujardin.

Secrétaire : Bonjour, bien sûr, je regarde ses disponibilités.
Secretary : Hello, of course, I'm looking at his availability.

Secrétaire : Demain à 15h00 cela vous irait ?
Secretary : Tomorrow at 3pm would that be okay ?

Patient : Vous n'avez pas plus tôt ?
Patient : Didn't you have earlier ?

Secrétaire : J'ai aujourd'hui mais c'est à 20h00 et il aura sûrement un peu de retard, c'est bon pour vous ?
Secretary : I have today but it's at 8pm and he'll probably be a little late, is that okay with you ?

Patient : Oui parfait ! Je vous remercie, à ce soir.
Patient : Yes, perfect ! Thank you, see you tonight.

Secrétaire : Bien, c'est noté.
Secretary : All right, noted.

Je vais chez le docteur.
I am going to the doctor.

J'ai mal au ventre.
My stomach hurts.

J'ai mal à la jambe.
My leg hurts.

Je crois que j'ai la grippe.
I think I have the flu.

Je tousse beaucoup.
I have a bad cough.

J'ai de la fièvre.
I have a fever.

J'ai la diarrhée depuis trois jours.
I have had diarrhea for three days.

J'ai mal à la tête.
I have a headache.

J'ai mal au bras.
My arm hurts.

Je suis enrhumé.
I have a cold.

J'ai les yeux secs.
My eyes are dry.

J'ai une toux sèche.
I have a dry cough.

Je suis constipé.
I have constipation.

J'ai vomi plusieurs fois.
I threw up several times.

Comment prendre rendez-vous chez le docteur ?
How do I make an appointment with the doctor ?

Sur quel site prendre rendez-vous ?
Which website do I use to make an appointment ?

Voici une ordonnance à donner au pharmacien.
Here is a prescription to give to the pharmacist.

Je vous conseille de prendre du Paracétamol deux fois par jour pendant une semaine.
I advise you to take Paracetamol twice a day for a week.

J'ai besoin de voir un docteur s'il vous plaît.
I need to see a doctor please.

C'est urgent, je dois voir un docteur.
It's urgent, I need to see a doctor.

À quelle heure le médecin est-il disponible ?
What time is the doctor available ?

Où puis-je aller voir le médecin ?
Where can I go to see the doctor ?

Je suis diabétique.
I have diabetes.

J'ai de l'hypertension.
I have high blood pressure.

Dois-je prendre le médicament avec la nourriture ?
Should I take the medication with food ?

Combien de fois par jour dois-je prendre le médicament ?
How many times a day should I take the medication ?

Prenez-vous des médicaments en ce moment ?
Are you currently taking any medications ?

Depuis combien de temps avez-vous ces symptômes ?
How long have you had these symptoms ?

Il vous faut une radio.
You need an x-ray.

Nous allons devoir vous poser un plâtre.
We will need to put a cast on you.

At the pharmacy

Bonjour, voici mon ordonnance.
Hello, here is my prescription.

Une pastille pour la toux.
A cough drop.

Combien de pilules dois-je prendre ?
How many pills should I take ?

Je cherche un médicament pour mon rhume.
I am looking for a cold medicine.

Je cherche un médicament contre les allergies.
I am looking for allergy medicine.

Est-ce que ce médicament s'utilise pour les enfants ?
Is this medicine for children ?

J'aimerais acheter de l'aspirine.
I would like to buy some aspirin.

Vendez-vous des tampons s'il vous plaît ?
Do you sell tampons please ?

Où se trouve la pharmacie la plus proche ?
Where is the nearest pharmacy ?

Bonjour, j'ai besoin d'un médicament contre le mal de tête.
Hello, I need a headache medicine.

Est-ce que vous avez quelque chose pour un coup de soleil ?

Do you have anything for sunburn ?

Vendez-vous des préservatifs ?
Do you sell condoms ?

À quelle heure ouvre la pharmacie ?
What time does the pharmacy open ?

À quelle heure ferme la pharmacie ?
What time does the pharmacy close ?

Combien de temps est-ce que je dois attendre ?
How long do I have to wait ?

J'ai besoin d'un anti-inflammatoire.
I need an anti-inflammatory.

Je prends la pilule.
I am on birth control pill.

J'ai la jambe dans le plâtre depuis deux mois.
My leg has been in a cast for two months.

Mon enfant a du mal à avaler les gros comprimés.
My child has trouble swallowing large tablets.

At the hospital

Emergency numbers to know

For a medical emergency, **you must call Samu by dialing "15" on your phone.**

To report a crime, **you must call the police by dialing "17" on your phone.**

To report an accident or a fire, **you must call the fire department by dialing "18" on your phone.**

Dans quelle chambre d'hôpital est ma fille ?
What hospital room is my daughter in ?

Puis-je voir une infirmière s'il vous plaît ?
Can I see a nurse please ?

À quelle heure ouvre l'hôpital ?
What time does the hospital open ?

Où est l'hôpital le plus proche s'il vous plaît ?
Where is the nearest hospital, please ?

C'est une urgence, à l'aide !
It's an emergency, help !

Le docteur va appeler un chirurgien spécialisé.
The doctor will call a specialist surgeon.

Sur une échelle de 1 à 10, comment noteriez-vous votre douleur ?
On a scale of 1 to 10, how would you rate your pain ?

Vous allez être transféré aux urgences.
You are being transferred to the emergency room.

Appuyez sur ce bouton pour appeler une infirmière.
Press this button to call a nurse.

Nous allons faire une analyse de sang.
We are going to do a blood test.

S'il vous plaît, veuillez attendre en salle d'attente.
Please wait in the waiting room.

Appelez une ambulance !
Call an ambulance !

Remplissez ces documents.
Fill out this paperwork.

Nous allons la transférer en soins intensifs.
We will transfer her to the ICU.

J'ai eu un accident
I had an accident

Il a perdu connaissance avant d'arriver à l'hôpital.
He lost consciousness before he got to the hospital.

Nous pensons qu'il a une hémorragie.
We think he is bleeding.

At the dentist

TIP : To find a doctor, a dentist or a health professional, I invite you to go to the reference site in the field : doctolib.fr.

This site allows you to easily book an appointment with any health professional for free ! You can even choose a professional who speaks your language.

Une dent	Une dent de lait
A tooth	A baby tooth

Une molaire
A molar

Une canine
A canine tooth

Une dent de devant
A front tooth

Les dents de sagesse
Wisdom teeth

La gencive
The gum

La mâchoire
The jaw

Il semblerait que vous ayez une carie.
It seems that you have a cavity.

J'aimerais un détartrage s'il vous plaît.
I would like a descaling please.

J'ai mal aux dents depuis cinq jours.
My tooth has been hurting for five days.

Je crois que ma dent du fond est cassée.
I think my back tooth is broken.

Pourrais-je avoir un blanchiment des dents ?
Could I have my teeth whitened ?

Je voudrais une visite de contrôle.
I would like a check-up.

Mes gencives saignent.
My gums are bleeding.

Quelle est la dent qui vous fait mal ?
Which tooth is causing you pain ?

Nous allons procéder à une dévitalisation de la dent.
We will proceed with a root canal on the tooth.

Je crois avoir un abcès.
I think I have an abscess.

Je crois avoir perdu une couronne.
I think I have lost a crown.

Pouvez-vous me donner quelque chose pour la douleur ?
Can you give me something for the pain ?

J'ai besoin de faire réparer mon dentier.
I need to get my dentures fixed.

Elle porte un appareil dentaire.
She wears braces.

Un de mes plombages est parti.
One of my fillings has come out.

Leisure activities

Tourism

Où est l'office du tourisme ?
Where is the tourist office ?

Quels monuments visiter à Paris ?
Which monuments to visit in Paris ?

Quelles activités recommandez-vous ?
What activities do you recommend ?

Proposez-vous une visite guidée ?
Do you offer a guided tour ?

Où est le musée du Louvre ?
Where is the Louvre Museum ?

À quelles heures ouvre le musée ?
What time does the museum open ?

Est-ce qu'il y a un prix réduit pour les touristes ?
Is there a reduced price for tourists ?

Quel est le chemin le plus rapide pour ce musée ?
What is the fastest way to this museum ?

Quelle attraction doit-on visiter ?
Which attraction should I visit ?

Combien coûte l'entrée pour ce musée ?
How much does it cost to enter this museum ?

Interests

Avez-vous une passion ?
Do you have a passion ?

Que faites-vous pendant votre temps libre ?
What do you do in your free time ?

Est-ce que la politique vous intéresse ?
Are you interested in politics ?

Regardez-vous beaucoup de films ?
Do you watch a lot of movies ?

Tu aimerais faire quoi ce week-end ?
What would you like to do this weekend ?

Quelles sont les activités préférées des Français ?
What are the favorite activities of the French ?

Aimez-vous voyager ?
Do you like to travel ?

Dans quels pays avez-vous voyagé ?
What countries have you traveled to ?

Vous aimeriez partir dans quel pays ?
What country would you like to travel to ?

J'adore écouter de la musique.
I love listening to music.

Ma passion est mon chien, il est trop mignon.

My passion is my dog, he is so cute.

Je fais de la poterie quand j'ai du temps libre.
I do pottery when I have free time.

Je veux aller au théâtre puis à l'opéra.
I want to go to the theater and then to the opera.

Ma grand-mère aime la couture.
My grandmother likes to sew.

Je collectionne les timbres.
I collect stamps.

Quel est ton humoriste préféré ?
Who is your favorite comedian ?

Combien de fois par mois allez-vous au cinéma ?
How many times a month do you go to the movies ?

J'adore cuisiner des gâteaux au chocolat.
I love to bake chocolate cakes.

Je suis un magicien, j'aime faire des tours de cartes.
I am a magician, I like to do card tricks.

Je m'occupe de mon potager tous les week-ends.
I take care of my garden every weekend.

Je suis un passionné d'investissement.
I am an investment enthusiast.

J'investis en Bourse tous les mois.
I invest in the stock market every month.

Je m'intéresse beaucoup à l'immobilier.
I am very interested in real estate.

J'observe les oiseaux pendant mon temps libre.
I watch birds in my free time.

J'adore jouer aux jeux vidéo quand j'ai le temps.
I love to play video games when I have time.

Mon fils programme sur son ordinateur, il fait des logiciels.
My son programs on his computer, he makes software.

Ma mère pratique la méditation pour se calmer.
My mother practices meditation to calm herself.

Nous faisons un match de foot tous les vendredis soir avec mes copains.
We have a soccer game every Friday night with my friends.

Je fais du tir à l'arc avec mon frère.
I do archery with my brother.

Je danse avec ma copine sur de la musique electro.
I dance with my girlfriend to electro music.

Je vais souvent à la pêche avec mon oncle.
I often go fishing with my uncle.

Ma petite amie joue de la guitare et moi du piano.
My girlfriend plays the guitar and I play the piano.

J'écoute de la musique sur mon téléphone.
I listen to music on my phone.

Mon livre préféré est un roman d'Agatha Christie.
My favorite book is an Agatha Christie novel.

Je fais de la dégustation de vins à Saint-Émilion.
I do wine tasting in Saint-Emilion.

Je joue aux échecs depuis que j'ai cinq ans.

I have been playing chess since I was five years old.

Avec mon père nous nous baladions à vélo le week-end.
My father and I used to ride our bikes on the weekends.

Mon grand-père avait l'habitude de chasser le dimanche.
My grandfather used to go hunting on Sundays.

J'aime sortir avec les copains.
I like to go out with my friends.

Nous chantons depuis notre plus tendre enfance.
We have been singing since we were little.

Sports

Quel sport faites-vous ?
What sport do you do ?

Vous faites du sport le week-end ?
Do you play sports on weekends ?

Quelle est ta discipline préférée aux Jeux Olympiques ?
What is your favorite sport in the Olympics ?

Tu as regardé le dernier match de foot ?
Did you watch the last soccer game ?

Veux-tu aller faire du vélo ?
Do you want to go cycling ?

Avez-vous déjà joué au tennis ?
Have you ever played tennis ?

Quel jour allez-vous à la piscine ?
What day do you go to the pool ?

Avez-vous déjà regardé une partie de baseball ?
Have you ever watched a baseball game ?

Aimez-vous regarder le rugby à la télévision ?
Do you like to watch rugby on TV ?

Faites-vous beaucoup de sport ?
Do you play a lot of sports ?

Vous vous considérez comme un sportif ?
Do you consider yourself a sportsman ?

J'adore jouer au football.
I love to play soccer.

Mon équipe de football préférée est Chealsea.
My favorite soccer team is Chelsea.

Je n'aime pas le baseball et le golf.
I don't like baseball and golf.

Mon jeu vidéo préféré est MarioKart.
My favorite video game is MarioKart.

J'ai fait du parapente à Annecy.
I went paragliding in Annecy.

Je suis un grand fan d'escalade.
I'm a big fan of rock climbing.

Nous faisons de la gymnastique à l'école.
We do gymnastics at school.

Chaque matin je fais mon footing avec mon amie.
Every morning I go jogging with my friend.

Je vais regarder un combat de boxe ce soir.
I'm going to watch a boxing match tonight.

J'ai parié cinquante euros sur mon équipe préférée.
I bet fifty euros on my favorite team.

Je joue au volley dans l'équipe féminine.
I play volleyball in the women's team.

Il fait beau, je vais aller faire un tour de vélo.
The weather is nice, I'm going to go for a bike ride.

Il s'est cassé le genou en allant au ski.
He broke his knee on the way to the ski resort.

Il y a un tournoi de tennis dans ma ville.

There is a tennis tournament in my town.

Je fais du tennis de temps en temps.
I play tennis from time to time.

Nous jouons souvent au basketball avec nos amis.
We often play basketball with our friends.

J'adore faire du cheval en forêt le week-end.
I love to ride horses in the forest on weekends.

Je joue au football tous les dimanches.
I play soccer every Sunday.

Shopping

France and luxury

France is the country of luxury ! Indeed, fashion is an important part of our culture and of our economy. Our biggest companies are in this sector, among the most famous companies in the luxury sector in France we find :

- Louis Vuitton
- Chanel
- Dior
- Cartier
- Hermès

So if you have a well-filled wallet... you have plenty to enjoy in France !

Color and sizes

Avez-vous la taille au-dessus pour ce modèle ?
Do you have the size up for this model ?

Avez-vous ces chaussures en taille 38 ?
Do you have these shoes in size 38 ?

Ces chaussures sont-elles disponibles en taille 42 ?

Are these shoes available in size 42 ?

Je vais faire du shopping dimanche, tu viens avec moi ?
I'm going shopping on Sunday, will you come with me ?

Je fais les magasins ce week-end, ça te dit de venir ?
I'm shopping this weekend, do you want to come ?

On va faire un tour aux Galeries Lafayette.
Let's go to Galeries Lafayette.

J'ai acheté ces chaussures la semaine dernière.
I bought these shoes last week.

Je suis jalouse, ta robe est si belle !
I'm jealous, your dress is so beautiful !

J'ai trouvé un magasin avec des vêtements abordables.
I found a store with affordable clothes.

Est-ce qu'il y a des soldes ?
Is there a sale ?

Est-ce que je peux avoir un sac ?
Can I have a bag ?

Vous cherchez quelque chose en particulier ?
Are you looking for anything in particular ?

Oui, je cherche un jean bleu.
Yes, I'm looking for blue jeans.

Est-ce que vous l'avez en M ?
Do you have it in medium size ?

Je voudrais voir cette robe mais en rouge.
I would like to see this dress but in red.

Est-ce qu'il y a un miroir ?
Is there a mirror ?

Où sont les cabines ?
Where are the booths ?

C'est trop serré !
It's too tight !

Tu devrais acheter cette jupe, elle te va super bien.
You should buy this skirt, it looks great on you.

Vous êtes ouvert les dimanches ?
Are you open on Sundays ?

Je cherche quelque chose de moins cher.
I'm looking for something cheaper.

Est-ce que cette jupe est en solde ?
Is this skirt on sale ?

Je vais essayer ce pull.
I'll try this sweater.

Ce t-shirt me plaît beaucoup.
I really like this shirt.

Je voudrais échanger cette chemise pour une autre taille, s'il vous plaît.
I would like to exchange this shirt for another size, please.

Ce n'est pas exactement ce que je veux.
This is not exactly what I want.

Je cherche ce pantalon en taille 38.
I am looking for these pants in size 38.

Avez-vous ce chemisier en taille 13 ?

Do you have this blouse in size 13 ?

Je vais essayer ce blouson.
I'm going to try this jacket.

Désolé, nous n'en avons pas.
Sorry, we don't have any.

Notre stock est épuisé.
We are out of stock.

Money and payment

Important : Save money

According to the European Commission : **"Visitors who leave the territory of the EU to return home or go to another non-EU country can buy goods VAT-free."**

VAT is a tax on all consumer goods that you buy. For a piece of clothing or a souvenir in a store, **the VAT amounts to 20% of the price of the object. So if you can deduct it**, you will save a lot of money !

To be eligible for VAT refund on your purchases, I invite you to consult the European Commission website to see the steps related to your situation. You can easily earn a few dozen or even hundreds of euros. So it's really worth it !

Y a-t-il une promotion de fin de saison ?
Is there an end of season promotion ?

Quand commenceront les soldes ?

When will the discounted sales start ?

Où est le magasin de vêtements le plus proche s'il vous plaît ?
Where is the nearest clothing store, please ?

Où puis-je trouver des vêtements pour hommes ?
Where can I find men's clothing ?

Puis-je payer par carte de crédit ?
Can I pay by credit card ?

Où est le bureau de change le plus proche ?
Where is the nearest exchange office ?

Je voudrais échanger des dollars contre des euros.
I would like to exchange dollars for euros.

Où puis-je retirer de l'argent ?
Where can I withdraw money ?

Où est le distributeur automatique le plus proche ?
Where is the nearest ATM ?

Combien coûte cette robe ?
How much does this dress cost ?

Où est la caisse s'il vous plaît ?
Where is the cash register please ?

Avez-vous une carte de fidélité ?
Do you have a loyalty card ?

Avez-vous appliqué la réduction ?
Did you apply the discount ?

J'aimerais régler en liquide s'il vous plaît.
I would like to pay cash please.

Quelle est votre politique pour les remboursements ?

What is your refund policy ?

Puis-je me faire rembourser ?
Can I get a refund ?

Useful questions and phrases

Avez-vous un numéro de téléphone ?
Do you have a phone number ?

Connaissez-vous un bon médecin ?
Do you know a good doctor ?

Avez-vous Messenger ou WhatsApp ?
Do you have Messenger or WhatsApp ?

Puis-je emprunter ceci ?
Can I borrow this ?

Puis-je avoir un reçu s'il vous plaît ?
Can I have a receipt please ?

Puis-je m'asseoir ici ?
May I sit here ?

Pourrais-je avoir votre attention s'il vous plaît ?
May I have your attention please ?

Avez-vous besoin de quelque chose ?
Is there anything you need ?

Je suis occupé cette semaine.
I'm busy this week.

Je suis impatient de travailler avec vous.
I look forward to working with you.

Veuillez m'excuser pour mon retard.
I apologize for being late.

C'était un plaisir de vous rencontrer.
It was a pleasure to meet you.

Merci beaucoup pour votre temps.
Thank you very much for your time.

Passez une belle journée.
Have a nice day.

Juste une minute s'il vous plaît.
Just a minute please.

Comment puis-je vous aider ?
How can I help you ?

Que faites-vous ici ?
What are you doing here ?

Que voulez-vous ?
What do you want ?

Qu'est-il arrivé ?
What has happened ?

Quand est le prochain arrêt ?
When is the next stop ?

Quelle est la température dehors ?
What is the temperature outside ?

Qui y va ?
Who is going ?

Ravi de faire votre connaissance.

Nice to meet you.

Va nettoyer ta chambre.
Go clean your room.

Je suis très occupé.
I am very busy.

Je n'ai pas le temps maintenant.
I don't have time now.

J'ai besoin de changer de vêtements.
I need to change my clothes.

J'ai besoin d'aller chez moi.
I need to go home.

Pourrais-je parler à Monsieur Dujardin s'il vous plaît ?
May I please speak to Monsieur Dujardin ?

S'il vous plaît remplissez ce formulaire.
Please fill out this form.

Ça sent mauvais.
It smells bad.

Pourriez-vous l'écrire ?
Could you write it down ?

Je ne connais pas ma taille.
I don't know my size.

Il est revenu d'Espagne en avril.
He came back from Spain in April.

C'est trop facile pour lui.
It's too easy for him.

J'ai acheté une baguette à la boulangerie.
I bought a baguette at the bakery.

C'est le livre dont je t'ai parlé.
This is the book I told you about.

Je préfère le poisson à la viande.
I prefer fish to meat.

Avez-vous une alternative végétarienne ?
Do you have a vegetarian alternative ?

J'ai reçu ton message.
I got your message.

Puis-je prendre votre voiture ?
Can I take your car ?

Où puis-je trouver un vélo ?
Where can I find a bike ?

J'ai une idée.
I have an idea.

J'ai perdu mon portefeuille.
I lost my wallet.

Avez-vous un peu de temps ?
Do you have some time ?

Avez-vous des frères ou des sœurs ?
Do you have brothers or sisters ?

Vous avez une brosse à dents pour moi ?
Do you have a toothbrush for me ?

À quelle heure vous levez-vous le matin ?
What time do you get up in the morning ?

Nous nous connaissons depuis huit ans.
We have known each other for eight years.

Avez-vous vu Monsieur Dujardin récemment ?
Have you seen Monsieur Dujardin recently ?

Quand je suis arrivé à la gare, le train était déjà parti.
When I arrived at the station, the train had already left.

Pouvez-vous venir me chercher au 3 rue Général Leclerc.
Can you pick me up at 3 rue Général Leclerc.

Je dois raccrocher.
I have to hang up.

Où pourrais-je rencontrer d'autres anglophones ?
Where can I meet other English speakers ?

Combien coûte une maison dans ce quartier ?
How much does a house cost in this neighborhood ?

Quel est le prix d'une voiture de location ?
How much does a rental car cost ?

Non désolé, je n'ai pas d'argent sur moi.
No sorry, I don't have any money on me.

C'est gratuit.
It's free.

C'est Noël.
It's Christmas.

BONUS: French expressions

The French love to use weird expressions ! In this part, I will teach you some expressions to look like a real Frenchman. Let's start right away :

Battre le fer pendant qu'il est chaud.
Strike the iron while it is hot.
Signification : Il faut vite profiter d'une situation

J'ai le cafard.
I have the cockroach.
Signification : J'ai très peur.

J'ai le coup de foudre pour toi.
I have a thunderbolt for you.
Signification : Je suis tombé amoureux de toi au premier regard.

Ce n'est pas la mer à boire.
It's not the sea to drink.
Signification : Ce n'est pas si impossible que ça.

Cet objet coûte les yeux de la tête.
This item costs the eyes of the head.
Signification : Ça coûte super cher.

Se prendre un râteau.
To hit a rake.
Signification : Quand une personne essaye d'en séduire une autre mais se fait rejeter.

La nuit porte conseil.

The night brings advice.
Signification : Il faut prendre du temps pour prendre la bonne décision.

Se faire rouler dans la farine.
Getting rolled in the flour.
Signification : Se faire arnaquer ou tromper par naïveté.

Poser un lapin à quelqu'un.
To put a rabbit to someone.
Signification : Abandonnez un rendez-vous sans prévenir la personne

L'habit ne fait pas le moine.
The outfit doesn't make the monk.
Signification : Il ne faut pas se fier aux apparences.

Casser les pieds à quelqu'un.
Breaking someone's feet.
Signification : Être très embêtant.

S'envoyer en l'air.
To throw oneself in the air.
Signification : Une expression familière pour "faire l'amour"

Mieux vaut tard que jamais.
Late is worth more than never.
Signification : Il est préférable de faire quelque chose en retard plutôt que de ne jamais le faire

Revenons à nos moutons.
Get back to our sheeps.
Signification : Revenons-en au sujet principal.

Avoir la pêche/banane/patate.
To have the peach/banana/potato.
Signification : Être en super forme.

Mieux vaut être seul que mal accompagné.

Better alone than in a bad company.
Signification : Il faut bien choisir ses amis, ses amours et ses proches.

En avoir ras-le-bol.
To have a full bowl.
Signification : En avoir assez

Crever la dalle.
To die the slab.
Signification : Avoir très très très faim

Après la pluie, vient le beau temps.
After the rain, comes the good weather.
Signification : Aux évènements tristes succèdent généralement des évènements joyeux

Avoir la flemme.
To have laziness.
Signification : Avoir l'envie de ne rien faire.

Avoir du pain sur la planche.
To have bread on the board.
Signification : Avoir beaucoup de tâches à accomplir.

Les murs ont des oreilles.
The walls have ears.
Signification : Attention, peut-être qu'on nous écoute.

Un de ces quatre matins.
One of these four mornings.
Signification : Un de ces jours.

Être canon.
To be canon.
Signification : Être séduisant

L'appétit vient en mangeant.
Appetite comes with eating.

Signification : Il faut commencer pour continuer.

Être bête comme ses pieds.
To be stupid as your feet.
Signification : Être vraiment stupide.

Être rouge comme une tomate.
To be red like a tomato.
Signification : Un rougissement très marqué.

S'occuper de ses oignons.
To take care of your own onions.
Signification : S'occuper de ses propres affaires.

Faire la grasse matinée.
To make the fatty morning.
Signification : Se lever tard.

Être crevé.
To be flat.
Signification : Être vraiment épuisé.

Raconter des salades.
To tell salads.
Signification : Dire des mensonges

Passer une nuit blanche.
To pass a white night.
Signification : Passer une nuit sans dormir.

Ne pas être dans son assiette.
Not to be in one's plate.
Signification : Ne pas se sentir très bien.

Tu me cours sur le haricot.
You run me on the bean.
Signification : Tu m'énerves.

Faire un froid de canard.
A cold of duck.
Signification : Il fait très froid.

Être au taquet.
To be at a piece of wood.
Signification : Être en forme et réactif.

Les chiens ne font pas des chats.
Dogs don't make cats.
Signification : On ressemble à ces parents.

Parler comme une vache espagnole.
To speak like a Spanish cow.
Signification : Parler très mal une langue étrangère

Avoir la gueule de bois.
To have the wooden face.
Signification : Avoir la bouche sèche et mal à la tête après avoir bu beaucoup d'alcool.

Il n'y a pas de quoi fouetter un chat.
There's no reason to whip the cat.
Signification : Ce n'est pas si grave.

Être riche comme Crésus.
As rich as Croesus.
Signification : Être très riche.

Avoir un chat dans la gorge.
To have a cat in the throat.
Signification : Avoir la voix enrouée, la gorge prise.

Avoir un QI d'huître.
To have the IQ of an oyster.
Signification : Être stupide.

Avoir un poil dans la main.
To have a hair in the hand.

Signification : Être paresseux.

Avoir les yeux plus gros que le ventre.
To have the eyes bigger than the belly.
Signification : Surestimer ses capacités à faire quelque chose.

Congratulations

Congratulations ! You have just read all the phrases used by the French in their daily lives. If I congratulate you, it's because many people pick up a book, but few go all the way through. I can't tell you the exact figures, but from what I've seen, **only 10% of readers read a book all the way through !** So if you've made it this far, you're part of a small, motivated elite. And I'm sure you will succeed in learning French and becoming fluent. All you have to do is not give up and practice the language every day to progress.

Soon, in just a few weeks, if you are regular, you will surely have enough vocabulary to go to France and speak with locals. And I want to reassure you, even if you think your accent is not perfect, the French love English speakers and are understanding.

You know, I had the chance to travel to Eastern European countries. In these countries, people are very introverted and it's hard to start a conversation. I'm not saying that it's good or bad, it's just their culture.

In France, you should know that we are rather open and extroverted and we see tourists in a good light. So yes, even if your French is not perfect, you can still come to our country to drink good red wine and eat cheese !

Now, I would like to ask you a little favor if you don't mind. If you liked this book, then I invite you to leave a little review on Amazon.

In 60 seconds it's done and I would be really happy to find out what you thought of this book. I've put a lot of effort, time and sweat (*and many cups of coffee*) into making sure that you get to know some everyday French phrases. So your opinion would really mean a lot to me, and I thank you.

Also, by giving your review, this book will be featured on Amazon and more people like you will have the chance to read it. It's a small action for you, but this small act can improve lives... and bring me closer to **my goal of helping 100'000 people discover French culture and language**. So I really count on you, your opinion is important and I thank you in advance.

Tips to keep progressing

As I've told you throughout the book, the most important thing is consistency. Some of my students work two hours a day on their French for a month and then stop. The result ? They give up because the workload is too heavy.

On the other hand, I have students who work about 10 minutes a day and have a much better level because they practice the French language regularly. So you can practice French as much as you want, if you can manage to spend an hour a day, fine, do it, you will progress quickly. But if you have a busy schedule that varies from day to day, then 5 or 10 minutes each day is recommended.

On the other hand, if you want to improve your French quickly, I recommend you consume a lot of content in that language... and preferably on different media. You can read, watch or listen to :

- Youtube videos
- Series
- Audiobooks
- Podcasts
- Short stories in French
- Instagram / TikTok / Facebook videos
- And much more...

By listening to French people speaking on different media, you can work on different aspects of the language such as spelling, vocabulary or pronunciation. For example, a Youtube video will be perfect to work on pronunciation as well as to discover the spoken French language *(which is a little different from the written language)*.

On the other hand, reading a short story in French will allow you to discover new words and to see the construction of sentences in more detail. In fact, the different media and platforms are complementary for your learning of French, and you should take advantage of it !

For the last word, I want to thank you for your interest in the French language. By the way, I invite you to download the free ebook I offer at the beginning of this book. By downloading this ebook, you will be on my email list *(you can unsubscribe at any time)*.

So don't worry, I'm not a spammer and I don't throw ads every day... no, instead I share little tips from time to time to help you learn French. So if you are really motivated ? I invite you to join my list.

It was a real pleasure to help you learn French.
Je vous souhaite tout le bonheur du monde !

Amicalement,
Raphaël Pesquet - *The French Guy*

~~$97.00~~ FREE BONUSES

GRAB YOUR FREE BONUSES NOW

- 7 French Short Stories You'll Want to Read
- 14 Common Mistakes In French Made By Beginners
- 21 Daily French Conversations to Learn French
- BONUS : Your Step-By-Step French Study Plan

Scan the QR code to claim your **free** bonus
Or
masterfrenchnow.com/freebonus

Copyright © 2022 Raphaël Pesquet

The content contained within this book may not be reproduced, duplicated or transmitted without direct written permission from the author or the publisher. Under no circumstances will any blame or legal responsibility be held against the publisher, or author, for any damages, reparation, or monetary loss due to the information contained within this book, either directly or indirectly.

Legal Notice : This book is copyright protected. It is only for personal use. You cannot amend, distribute, sell, use, quote or paraphrase any part, or the content within this book, without the consent of the author or publisher.

Disclaimer Notice : Please note the information contained within this document is for educational and entertainment purposes only. All effort has been executed to present accurate, up to date, reliable, complete information. No warranties of any kind are declared or implied. Readers acknowledge that the author is not engaged in the rendering of legal, financial, medical or professional advice. The content within this book has been derived from various sources. Please consult a licensed professional before attempting any techniques outlined in this book

By reading this document, the reader agrees that under no circumstances is the author responsible for any losses, direct or indirect, that are incurred as a result of the use of the information contained within this document, including, but not limited to, errors, omissions, or inaccuracies.

END

Made in the USA
Monee, IL
29 December 2024

75637717R00066